Eau de Parfum

Size: 5⅜ inches W x 6¼ inches H (13.6cm x 15.9cm) excluding ribbon hanger, towel and embellishments
Skill Level: Beginner

Materials

- ❑ 1 sheet clear 7-count plastic canvas
- ❑ Red Heart Super Saver Art. E300 medium weight yarn as listed in color key
- ❑ Uniek Needloft metallic craft cord as listed in color key
- ❑ Uniek Needloft iridescent craft cord as listed in color key
- ❑ DMC 6-strand embroidery floss as listed in color key
- ❑ Sewing thread: white, gold
- ❑ 1 yard (1m) ⅝-inch-wide (15mm) pale green satin ribbon
- ❑ 2-inch (5.1cm) white pompom
- ❑ Lost & Found vintage Paris map pendant from Blue Moon Beads
- ❑ 65 (6mm) white pearl beads
- ❑ ½ yard (0.5m) silver 24-gauge beading wire
- ❑ Complementary hand towel
- ❑ Wire cutters or craft nippers
- ❑ Hand-sewing needle
- ❑ #16 tapestry needle

Project Note

Stitch using #16 tapestry needle unless instructed otherwise.

Stitching Step by Step

1 Cut front, back and pump from plastic canvas according to graphs.

2 Stitch front, back and pump according to graphs, filling in uncoded areas on front and back with cornmeal Continental Stitches.

3 When background stitching is complete, Backstitch and Straight Stitch pump and front using 3 strands dark gray embroidery floss.

4 Using white/silver metallic craft cord, Overcast edges of pump. Using gold yarn throughout, Overcast bottom edges of front and back, and top edges between arrows. Whipstitch front to back, wrong sides facing, along remaining edges.

5 Using sewing needle and gold thread and referring to photo throughout, center and stitch bottom edge of pump to top edge of towel topper front.

Embellishments & Finishing

1 Using sewing needle and white thread, stitch one end of a 6-inch (15.2cm) piece of white iridescent craft cord to pompom; stitch the other end to reverse side of pump near top. Tack pompom to front of towel topper along right-hand edge as shown.

2 Using sewing needle and gold thread, stitch pendant to front along left side as shown.

3 String pearls on wire; twist ends together and clip excess. Drape pearls over upper left-hand corner of towel topper as shown; using sewing needle and gold thread, tack ends to back of towel topper; tack pearls to front.

4 Fold towel in half over center of ribbon; thread ribbon ends through towel topper from bottom to top and tie in a bow. Trim ribbon ends as needed.

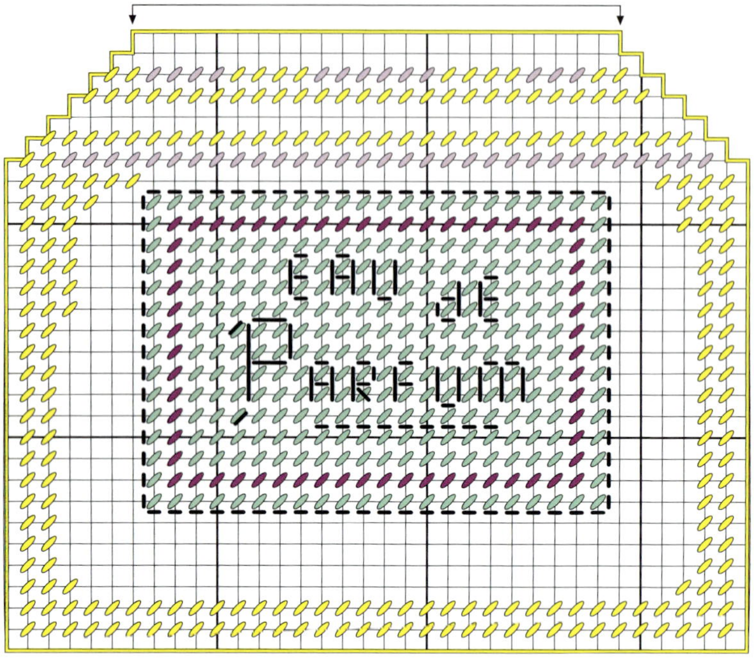

Eau de Parfum Front
35 holes x 29 holes
Cut 1

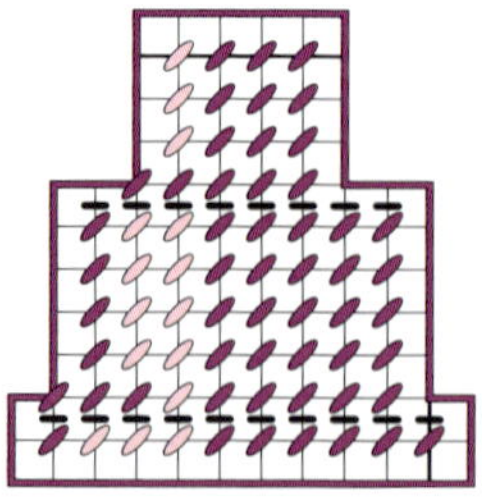

Eau de Parfum Pump
11 holes x 11 holes
Cut 1

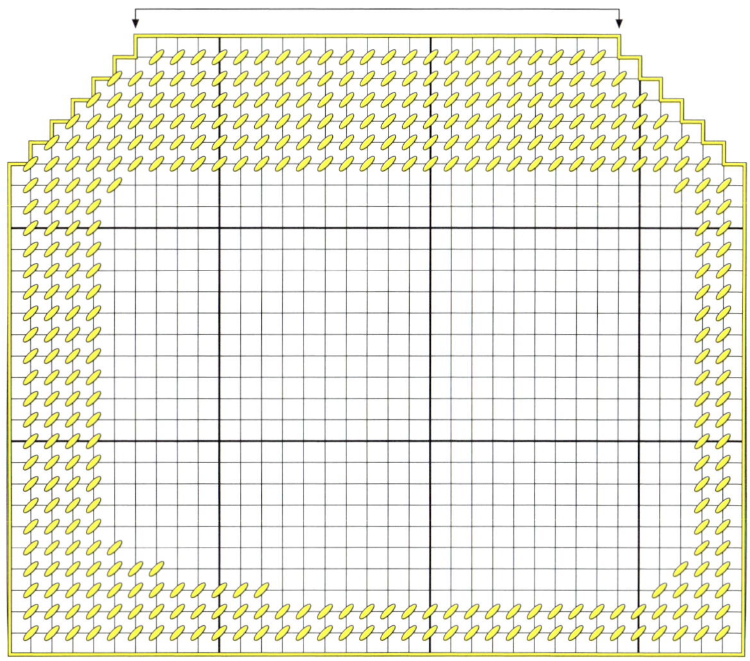

Eau de Parfum Back
35 holes x 29 holes
Cut 1

COLOR KEY

Yards	Medium Weight Yarn
1 (1m)	Aran #313
20 (18.3m)	Gold #321
5 (4.6m)	Pale green #363
20 (18.3m)	Uncoded areas are cornmeal #320 Continental Stitches
	Metallic Craft Cord
2 (1.9m)	White/silver #55008
	Iridescent Craft Cord
1 (1m)	White #55033
	6-Strand Embroidery Floss
2 (1.9m)	/ Dark gray #844 (3-ply) Backstitch and Straight Stitch

Color numbers given are for Red Heart Super Saver Art. E300 medium weight yarn, Uniek Needloft metallic and iridescent craft cord, and DMC 6-strand embroidery floss.

Bath Powder

Size: 5⅜ inches W x 4½ inches H (13.6cm x 11.4cm) excluding ribbon hanger, towel and embellishments
Skill Level: Beginner

Materials

- ❑ 1 sheet clear 7-count plastic canvas
- ❑ Red Heart Super Saver Art. E300 medium weight yarn as listed in color key
- ❑ Uniek Needloft metallic craft cord as listed in color key
- ❑ DMC 6-strand embroidery floss as listed in color key
- ❑ Sewing thread: pink, black
- ❑ 1 yard (1m) ⅜-inch-wide (9mm) peach/brown/pink dots ribbon from Offray
- ❑ Stylish Accents 1¼-inch x 1⅛-inch (3.3cm x 2.9cm) black ribbon flower bow from Offray
- ❑ 7 (1-inch/25mm) pink pompoms
- ❑ Complementary hand towel
- ❑ Hand-sewing needle
- ❑ #16 tapestry needle

Project Note

Stitch using #16 tapestry needle unless instructed otherwise.

Stitching Step by Step

1 Cut two pieces for front and back from plastic canvas according to graph.

2 Stitch front according to graph, filling in uncoded areas in center and at top with petal pink Continental Stitches.

3 For back, continue pattern of soft white and Aran stripes through center area; fill in uncoded area at top with petal pink Continental Stitches.

4 *When background stitching is complete, work embroidery on front:* Backstitch lettering using 3 strands dark brown embroidery floss. Straight Stitch flower leaves around oval using frosty green yarn. Work French Knot flowers around oval using ranch red yarn, wrapping yarn once around needle for each knot.

5 Using soft white yarn, Overcast bottom edges of front and back. Using petal pink yarn, Overcast top edges of front and back between arrows. Using soft white and petal pink yarn according to graph, Whipstitch front to back, wrong sides facing, along remaining edges.

Embellishments & Finishing

1 Using sewing needle and pink thread, stitch pompoms close together in a row along top edge of topper front. Using sewing needle and black thread, stitch ribbon flower bow to center pompom.

2 Fold towel in half over center of ribbon; thread ribbon ends through towel topper from bottom to top and tie in a bow. Trim ribbon ends as needed.

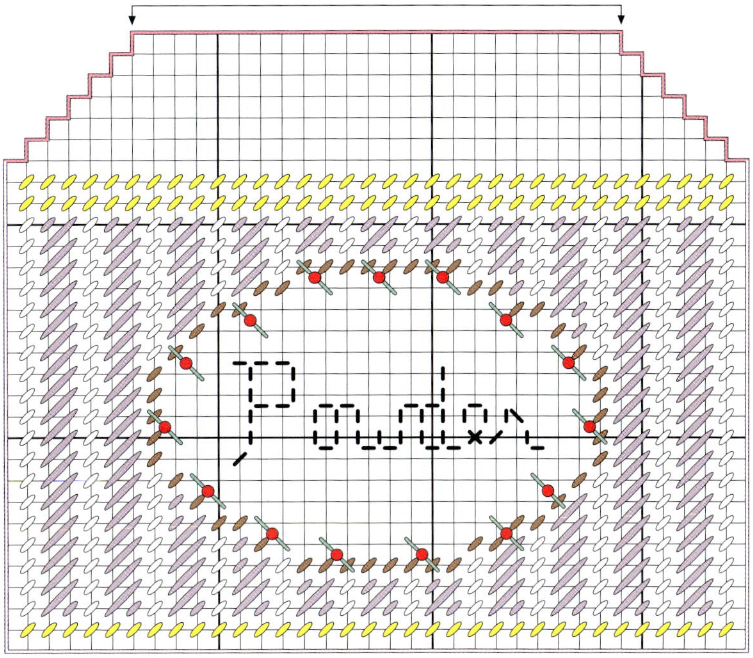

Bath Powder Front/Back
35 holes x 29 holes
Cut 2
Stitch 1 as shown for front
Stitch 1 replacing center oval with striped pattern for back

COLOR KEY

Yards	Medium Weight Yarn
12 (11m)	☐ Aran #313
15 (13.8m)	☐ Soft white #316
2 (1.9m)	■ Linen #330
20 (18.3m)	Uncoded areas are petal pink #373 Continental Stitches
	⁄ Petal pink #373 Overcast and Whipstitch
2 (1.9m)	⁄ Frosty green #661 Straight Stitch
2 (1.9m)	● Ranch red #332 (1-wrap) French Knot
	Metallic Craft Cord
5 (4.6m)	☐ Gold #55001
	6-Strand Embroidery Floss
1 (1m)	⁄ Dark brown #838 (3-ply) Backstitch

Color numbers given are for Red Heart Super Saver Art. E300 medium weight yarn, Uniek Needloft metallic craft cord and DMC 6-strand embroidery floss.

Pepper

Size: 5⅜ inches W x 4¾ inches H (13.6cm x 12.1cm) excluding ribbon hanger, towel and embellishments
Skill Level: Beginner

Materials

- ❑ 1 sheet clear 7-count plastic canvas
- ❑ Red Heart Super Saver Art. E300 medium weight yarn as listed in color key
- ❑ Uniek Needloft metallic craft cord as listed in color key
- ❑ DMC 6-strand embroidery floss as listed in color key
- ❑ Sewing thread: black, bright yellow
- ❑ Ribbon:
  - 1 yard (1m) ⅝-inch-wide (15mm) black-and-white polka-dot
  - 2 inches (5.1cm) ⅝-inch-wide (15mm) bright yellow double-sided satin
- ❑ Approximately 50 black seed beads
- ❑ Complementary dish towel or hand towel
- ❑ Hand-sewing needle
- ❑ #16 tapestry needle

Project Note

Stitch using #16 tapestry needle unless instructed otherwise.

Stitching Step by Step

1 Cut front and back from plastic canvas according to graphs. Also cut two squares 7 holes x 7 holes for butter pats.

2 Stitch front according to graph, filling in uncoded areas with warm brown Continental Stitches.

3 Fill in topper back with white Slanted Gobelin Stitches. Fill in butter pats with bright yellow Continental Stitches, Overcasting edges as you stitch.

4 When background stitching is complete, Backstitch potato on front using 3 strands dark brown embroidery floss.

5 Using white yarn, Overcast bottom edges of front and back; Overcast top edges between arrows.

Embellishments & Finishing

1 Referring to photo throughout and using sewing needle and bright yellow thread, tack bright yellow ribbon to potato as shown, turning under edges to form a "puddle" of "melted butter."

2 Using sewing needle and black thread, stitch seed beads randomly to front for pepper.

3 Using sewing needle and bright yellow thread, stitch butter pats to lower right portion of topper front as shown.

4 Using white yarn, Whipstitch front to back, wrong sides facing, along remaining edges.

5 Fold towel in half over center of ribbon; thread ribbon ends through towel topper from bottom to top and tie in a bow. Trim ribbon ends as needed.

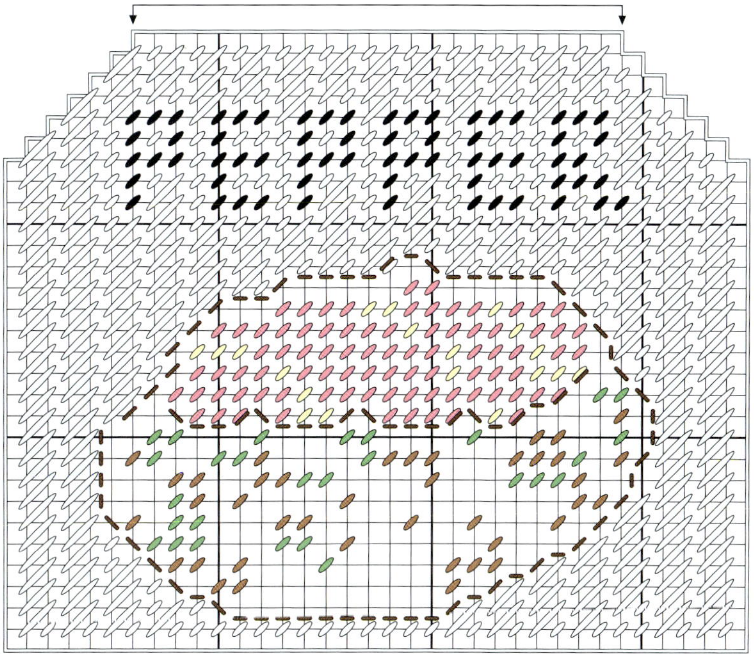

"Pepper" Front/Back
35 holes x 29 holes
Cut 2
Stitch 1 as shown for front
Stitch 1 completely in white Slanted Gobelin Stitches for back

COLOR KEY

Yards	Medium Weight Yarn
30 (27.5m)	☐ White #311
3 (2.8m)	■ Aran #313
2 (1.9m)	☐ Pale yellow #322
3 (2.8m)	Bright yellow #324
2 (1.9m)	■ Buff #334
2 (1.9m)	■ Coffee #365
5 (4.6m)	Uncoded areas are warm brown #336 Continental Stitches
	Metallic Craft Cord
2 (1.9m)	■ Black #55000
	6-Strand Embroidery Floss
1 (1m)	⁄ Dark brown #838 (3-ply) Backstitch

Color numbers given are for Red Heart Super Saver Art. E300 medium weight yarn, Uniek Needloft metallic craft cord and DMC 6-strand embroidery floss.

Salt

Size: 5⅜ inches W x 4¾ inches H (13.6cm x 12.1cm) excluding ribbon hanger, towel and embellishments

Skill Level: Beginner

Materials

- ❑ 1 sheet clear 7-count plastic canvas
- ❑ 2 (3-inch) plastic canvas radial circles from Uniek
- ❑ Uniek Needloft craft plastic canvas yarn as listed in color key
- ❑ Red Heart Super Saver Art. E300 medium weight yarn as listed in color key
- ❑ Uniek Needloft metallic craft cord as listed in color key
- ❑ Uniek Needloft iridescent craft cord as listed in color key
- ❑ DMC 6-strand embroidery floss as listed in color key
- ❑ White sewing thread
- ❑ 1 yard (1m) ⅝-inch-wide (15mm) black with white polka dots grosgrain ribbon
- ❑ Approximately 90 clear glass seed beads
- ❑ Complementary dish towel or hand towel
- ❑ Hand-sewing needle
- ❑ #16 tapestry needle

Project Note

Stitch using #16 tapestry needle unless instructed otherwise.

Stitching Step by Step

1 Cut front and back from 7-count plastic canvas according to graphs.

2 Cut two eggs from plastic canvas radial circles according to graph, cutting away gray areas.

Eggs

1 Stitch eggs according to graphs, Overcasting edges with white as you stitch.

2 Using sewing needle and white thread, stitch beads randomly to eggs, reserving 40–45 beads for towel topper.

Topper

1 Stitch front according to graph, filling in uncoded areas with white Continental Stitches.

2 When background stitching is complete, Backstitch salt shaker using 3 strands gray embroidery floss.

3 Using black yarn through step 4, fill in topper back with Slanted Gobelin Stitches.

4 Overcast bottom edges of front and back; Overcast top edges between arrows.

Embellishments & Finishing

1 Referring to photo and using sewing needle and white thread throughout, stitch eggs to topper front. Stitch reserved beads randomly to topper front for salt.

2 Using black yarn, Whipstitch front to back, wrong sides facing, along remaining edges.

3 Fold towel in half over center of ribbon; thread ribbon ends through towel topper from bottom to top and tie in a bow. Trim ribbon ends as needed.

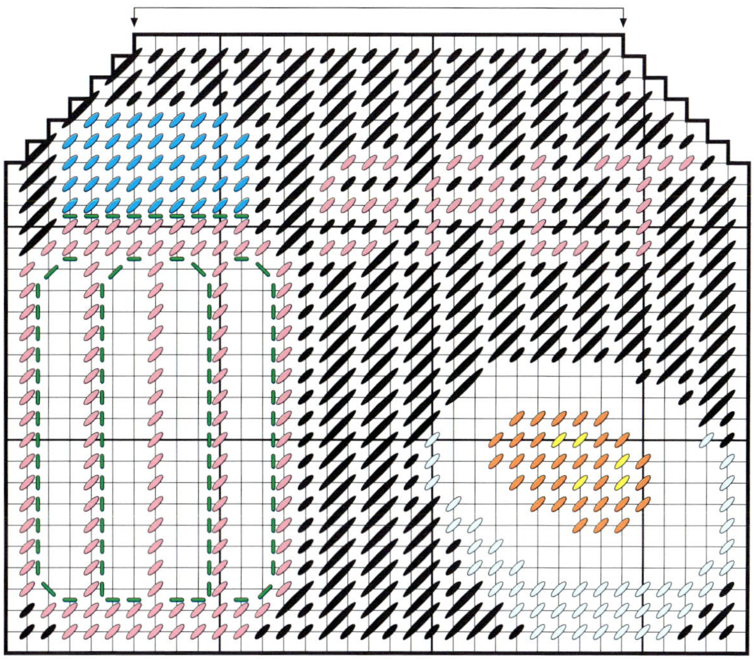

"Salt" Front/Back
35 holes x 29 holes
Cut 2
Stitch 1 as shown for front
Stitch 1 completely in black Slanted Gobelin Stitches for back

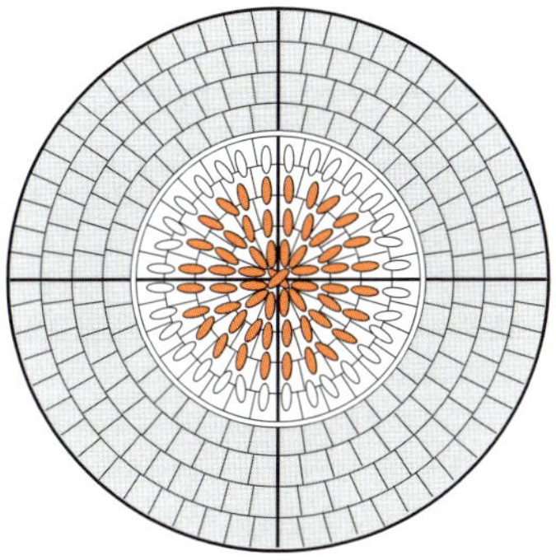

Egg
Cut 2 from 3-inch radial circles,
cutting away gray areas

COLOR KEY

Yards	
	Plastic Canvas Yarn
1 (1m)	☐ Silver #37
5 (4.6m)	Uncoded areas are white #41 Continental Stitches
	White #41 Overcast
	Medium Weight Yarn
30 (27.5m)	■ Black #312
3 (2.8m)	■ Cornmeal #320
1 (1m)	■ Pale yellow #322
	Metallic Craft Cord
2 (1.9m)	■ White/silver #55008
	Iridescent Craft Cord
5 (4.6m)	■ White #55033
	6-Strand Embroidery Floss
1 (1m)	Gray #414 (3-ply) Backstitch

Color numbers given are for Uniek Needloft plastic canvas yarn, and metallic and iridescent craft cord; Red Heart Super Saver Art. E300 medium weight yarn and DMC 6-strand embroidery floss.

"His"

Size: 6 inches W x 5 inches H x 2 inches D (15.3cm x 12.7cm x 5.1cm) excluding ribbon hanger and towel
Skill Level: Beginner

Materials

- ❑ 1 sheet clear 7-count plastic canvas
- ❑ 3 (3-inch) plastic canvas radial circles from Uniek
- ❑ Uniek Needloft plastic canvas yarn as listed in color key
- ❑ Red Heart Super Saver Art. E300 medium weight yarn as listed in color key
- ❑ Uniek Needloft iridescent craft cord as listed in color key
- ❑ Sewing thread: light brown, white
- ❑ 1 yard (1m) ⅜-inch-wide (9mm) blue/brown checks ribbon from Offray
- ❑ 9 (1-inch/25mm) white pompoms
- ❑ Complementary hand towel
- ❑ Hand-sewing needle
- ❑ #16 tapestry needle

Project Note

Stitch using #16 tapestry needle unless instructed otherwise.

Stitching Step by Step

1 Cut two pieces for front and back, one mug and one brush handle from 7-count plastic canvas according to graphs. Also cut one piece 3 holes x 18 holes for mug handle.

2 Cut mug base, brush base and brush bristles from plastic canvas radial circles according to graphs, cutting away gray areas.

Shaving Mug

1 Stitch mug and mug base according to graphs, filling in uncoded areas with camel Continental Stitches. Stitch mug handle completely in white Continental Stitches, Overcasting as you stitch.

2 Using white yarn, Whipstitch bottom edge of mug to curved edge of mug base; Overcast top edge of mug and back edges of mug and mug base.

3 Using sewing needle and white thread and referring to photo throughout, stitch ends of handle to mug top and bottom near left edge.

Brush

1 Stitch brush handle and brush base according to graphs, filling in uncoded areas with camel Continental Stitches.

2 Referring to diagram for Lark's Head Knot, page 12, fill mug bristles piece with Lark's Head Knots according to graph using 4½-inch (11.4cm) strands of Aran fleck yarn. Trim bristles evenly to 1¾ inches (4.4cm). Overcast edges.

3 Using camel yarn throughout, Whipstitch bottom edge of brush handle to curved edge of brush base; Whipstitch top edge of brush handle to curved edge of bristles. Overcast back edges of brush handle and base.

Towel Topper

1 Stitch front according to graph. Using white yarn, fill in back with Continental Stitches.

2 When background stitching is complete, Backstitch between white and iridescent white stitches on front using 3 strands brown-gray embroidery floss.

3 Using white yarn throughout, Overcast bottom edges of front and back. Overcast top edges of front and back between arrows.

Finishing

1 Using sewing needle and white thread, stitch shaving mug to topper where indicated by left-hand blue line on graph. Stitch pompoms to top of mug and towel topper for "shaving cream."

2 Using sewing needle and light brown thread, stitch shaving brush to topper where indicated by right-hand blue line on graph.

3 Using white yarn, Whipstitch front to back, wrong sides facing, along unfinished side edges.

4 Fold towel in half over center of ribbon; thread ribbon ends through towel topper from bottom to top and tie in a bow. Trim ribbon ends as needed.

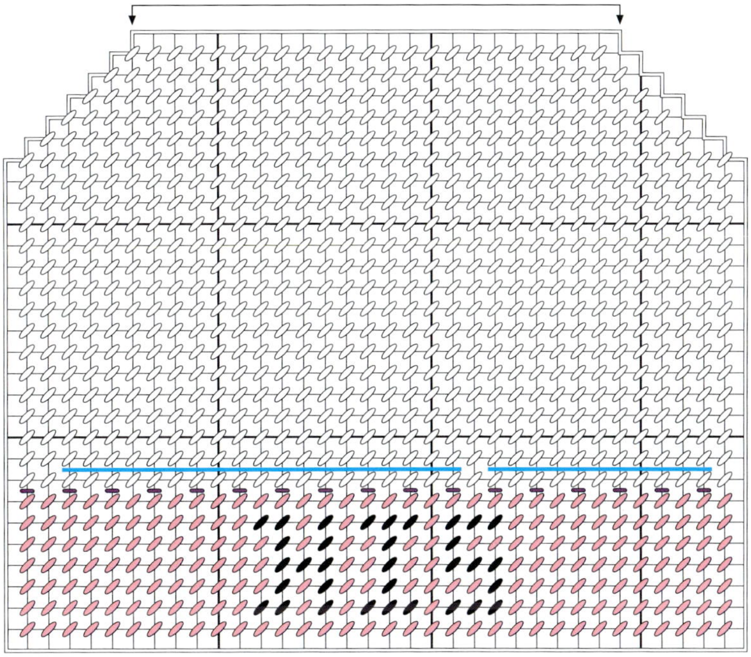

"His" Front/Back
35 holes x 29 holes
Cut 2
Stitch 1 as shown for front
Stitch 1 completely in white Continental Stitches for back

COLOR KEY

Yards	Plastic Canvas Yarn
1 (1m)	■ Black #00
4 (3.7m)	■ Cinnamon #14
1 (1m)	■ Sandstone #16
10 (9.2m)	□ White #41
6 (5.5m)	□ Camel #43
	Uncoded areas are camel #43 Continental Stitches
	Medium Weight Yarn
32 (29.3m)	□ White #311
8 (7.4m)	● Aran fleck #4313 Lark's Head Knot
	Iridescent Craft Cord
5 (4.6m)	□ White #55033
	6-Strand Embroidery Floss
1 (1m)	⁄ Brown-gray #452 (3-ply) Backstitch

Color numbers given are for Uniek Needloft plastic canvas yarn and iridescent craft cord, Red Heart Super Saver Art. E300 medium weight yarn and DMC 6-strand embroidery floss.

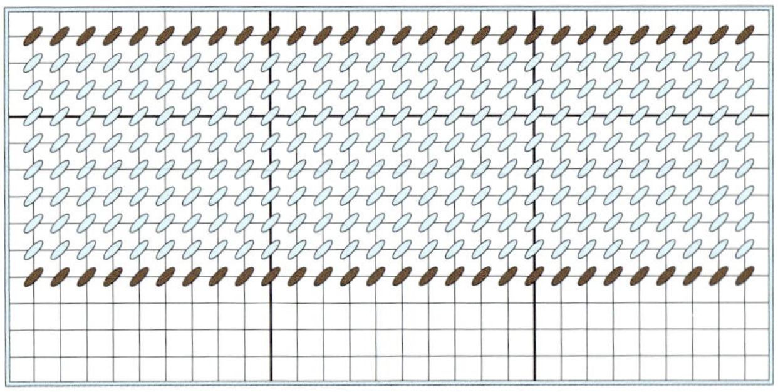

"His" Shaving Mug
29 holes x 14 holes
Cut 1

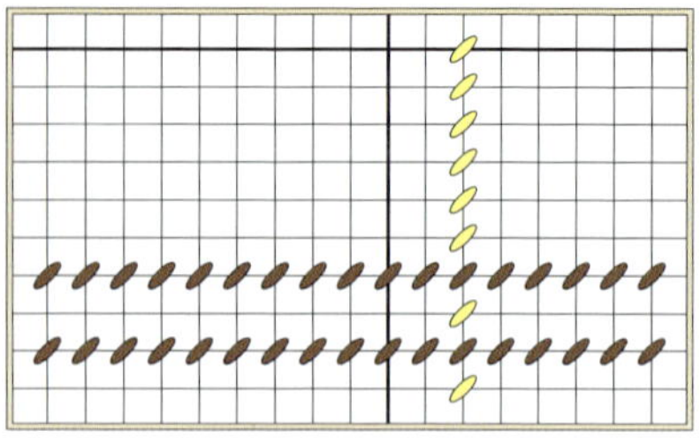

"His" Brush Handle
18 holes x 11 holes
Cut 1

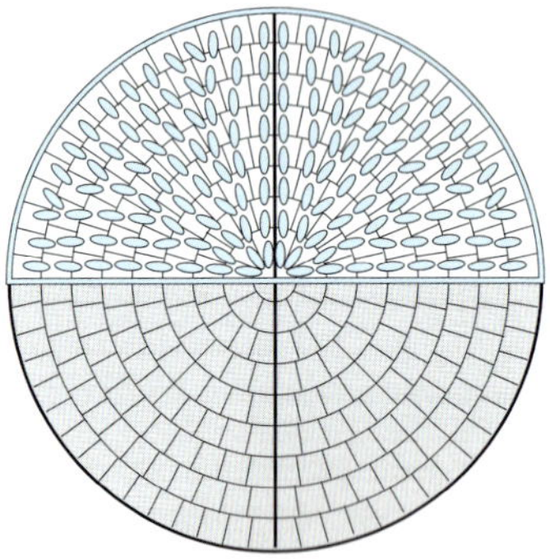

"His" Mug Base
Cut 1 from 3-inch radial circle,
cutting away gray areas

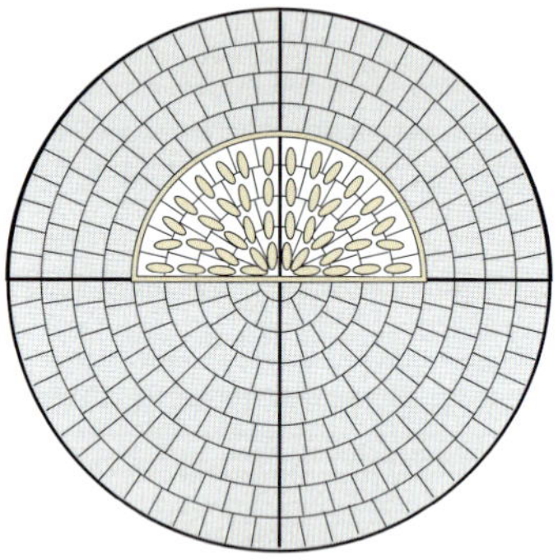

"His" Brush Base
Cut 1 from 3-inch radial circle,
cutting away gray areas

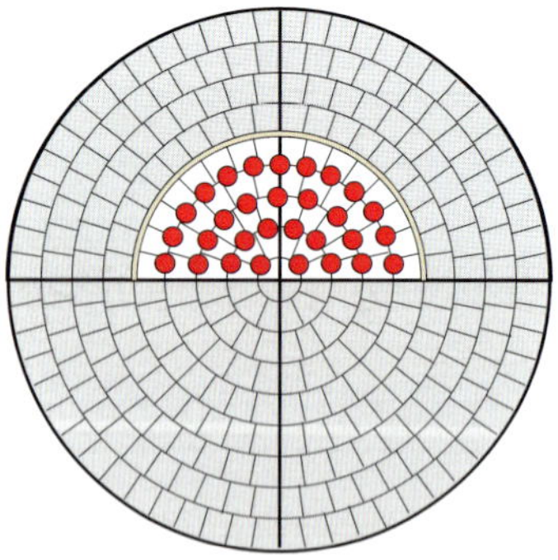

"His" Brush Bristles
Cut 1 from 3-inch radial circle,
cutting away gray areas

COLOR KEY

Yards	Plastic Canvas Yarn
1 (1m)	■ Black #00
4 (3.7m)	■ Cinnamon #14
1 (1m)	□ Sandstone #16
10 (9.2m)	□ White #41
6 (5.5m)	□ Camel #43
	Uncoded areas are camel #43 Continental Stitches
	Medium Weight Yarn
32 (29.3m)	□ White #311
8 (7.4m)	● Aran fleck #4313 Lark's Head Knot
	Iridescent Craft Cord
5 (4.6m)	□ White #55033
	6-Strand Embroidery Floss
1 (1m)	/ Brown-gray #452 (3-ply) Backstitch

Color numbers given are for Uniek Needloft plastic canvas yarn and iridescent craft cord, Red Heart Super Saver Art. E300 medium weight yarn and DMC 6-strand embroidery floss.

Fig. 1
Lark's Head Knot

"Hers"

Size: 6 inches W x 5¼ inches H x 1½ inches D (15.2cm x 13.3cm x 3.8cm) excluding ribbon hanger and towel
Skill Level: Beginner

Materials

- ❑ 1 sheet clear 7-count plastic canvas
- ❑ 2 (3-inch) plastic canvas radial circles from Uniek
- ❑ Uniek Needloft plastic canvas yarn as listed in color key
- ❑ Red Heart Super Saver Art. E300 medium weight yarn as listed in color key
- ❑ Uniek Needloft iridescent craft cord as listed in color key
- ❑ DMC 6-strand embroidery floss as listed in color key
- ❑ Sewing thread: brown, white
- ❑ 1 yard (1m) ⅜-inch-wide (9mm) peach/brown ribbon with pink dots from Offray
- ❑ ½-inch (12mm) cream ribbon rose
- ❑ 16 (3mm) white pearl beads
- ❑ Complementary hand towel
- ❑ Hand-sewing needle
- ❑ #16 tapestry needle

Project Note

Stitch using #16 tapestry needle unless instructed otherwise.

Stitching Step by Step

1 Cut two pieces for front and back, one comb and one brush handle from 7-count plastic canvas according to graphs.

2 Cut brush head and brush bristles from plastic canvas radial circles according to graphs, cutting away gray areas.

Comb

1 Stitch comb according to graph.

2 When background stitching is complete, Backstitch comb using cinnamon yarn. Without cutting yarn, Overcast spine of comb according to graph. Overcast remaining edges using sandstone yarn.

3 Using sewing needle and white thread, stitch pearl beads to edge of comb where indicated by blue dots on graph. Referring to photo throughout, center and stitch ribbon rose to comb in open space between pearls.

Brush

1 Stitch brush handle and brush head according to graphs, filling in uncoded areas on handle only with cinnamon Continental Stitches. Overcast edges of handle with brown and brush head with cinnamon.

2 Referring to diagram for Lark's Head Knot, page 12, fill brush bristles piece with Lark's Head Knots according to graph using 3-inch (7.6cm) strands of Aran fleck yarn. Trim bristles evenly to ¾ inch (2cm). Overcast edges with camel.

3 Using sewing needle and brown thread throughout, center and Whipstitch brush bristles to right side of brush head. Whipstitch right side of handle to wrong side of brush head, overlapping pieces as shown.

Towel Topper

1 Stitch front according to graph.

2 When background stitching is complete, Backstitch front using 3 strands light brown-gray embroidery floss.

3 Using white yarn through step 4, fill in back with Continental Stitches.

4 Overcast bottom edges of front and back. Overcast top edges of front and back between arrows.

Finishing

1 Using sewing needle and brown thread, tack brush and comb to topper front as shown.

2 Using white yarn, Whipstitch front to back, wrong sides facing, along unfinished side edges.

3 Fold towel in half over center of ribbon; thread ribbon ends through towel topper from bottom to top and tie in a bow. Trim ribbon ends as needed.

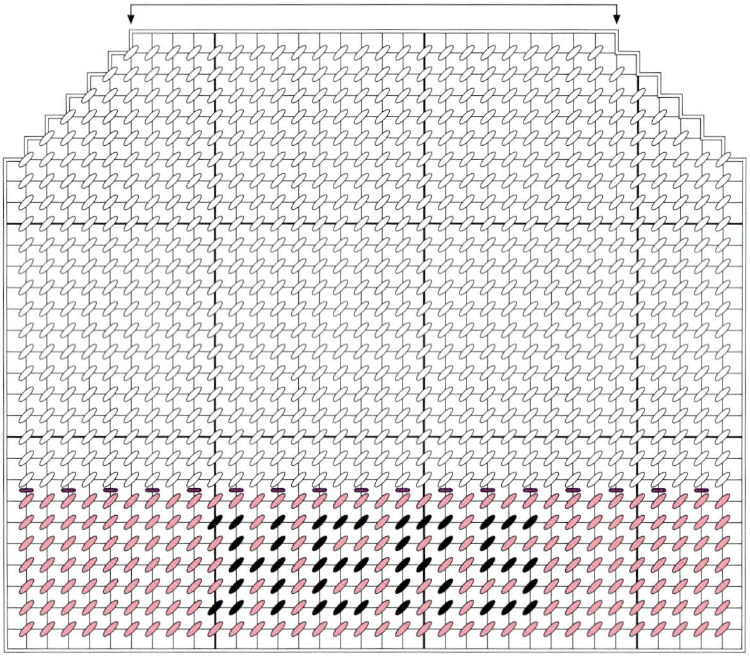

"Hers" Front/Back
35 holes x 29 holes
Cut 2
Stitch 1 as shown for front
Stitch 1 completely in white Continental Stitches for back

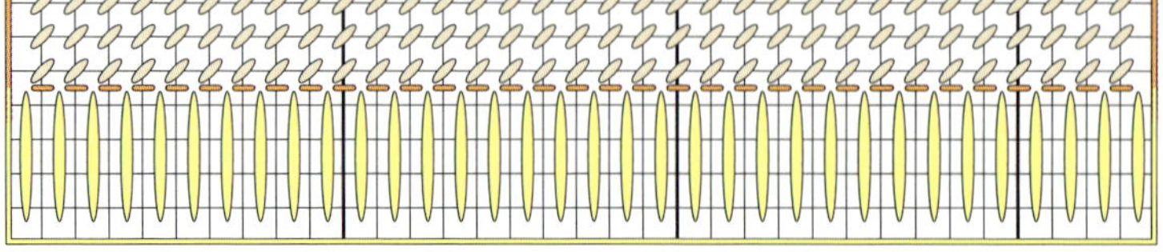

"Hers" Comb
34 holes x 8 holes
Cut 1

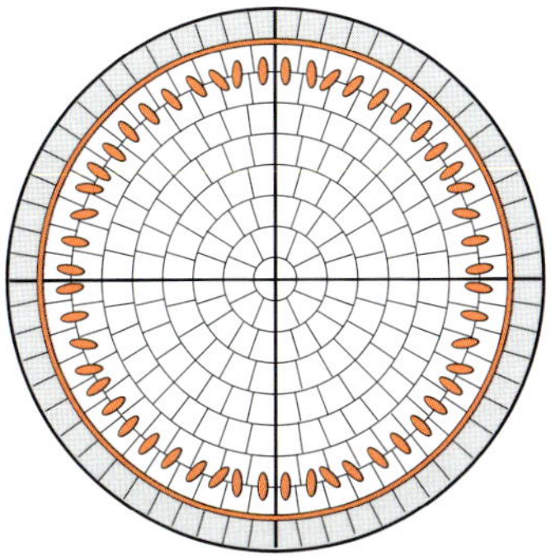

"Hers" Brush Head
Cut 1 from 3-inch radial circle,
cutting away gray areas

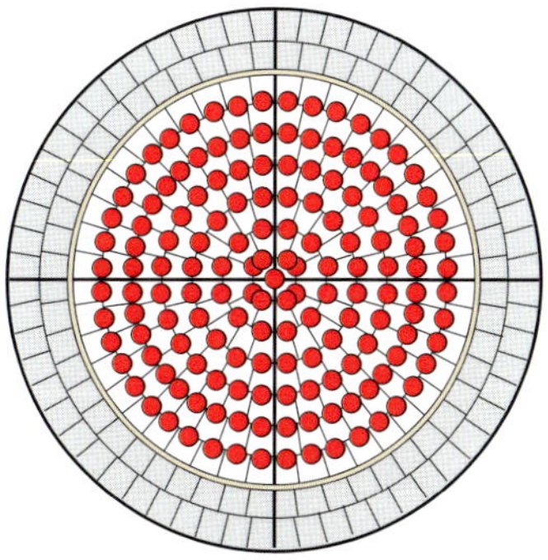

"Hers" Brush Bristles
Cut 1 from 3-inch radial circle,
cutting away gray areas

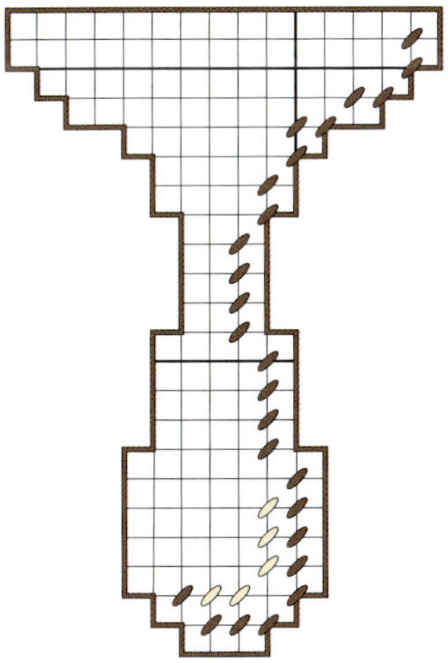

"Hers" Brush Handle
15 holes x 22 holes
Cut 1

COLOR KEY

Yards	Plastic Canvas Yarn
1 (1m)	■ Black #00
8 (7.4m)	■ Cinnamon #14
4 (3.7m)	■ Brown #15
3 (2.8m)	■ Sandstone #16
32 (29.3m)	□ White #41
5 (4.6m)	■ Camel #43
	Uncoded areas are cinnamon #14 Continental Stitches
	⁄ Cinnamon #14 Backstitch
	Medium Weight Yarn
32 (29.3m)	□ White #311
18 (16.5m)	● Aran fleck #4313 Lark's Head Knot
	Iridescent Craft Cord
5 (4.6m)	■ White #55033
	6-Strand Embroidery Floss
1 (1m)	⁄ Light brown-gray #452 (3-ply) Backstitch
	● Attach pearl bead

Color numbers given are for Uniek Needloft plastic canvas yarn and iridescent craft cord, Red Heart Super Saver Art. E300 medium weight yarn and DMC 6-strand embroidery floss.

Honey

Size: 5⅜ inches W x 4½ inches H (13.6cm x 11.4cm) excluding ribbon hanger, towel and lace trim.
Skill Level: Beginner

Materials

- ❑ 1 sheet clear 7-count plastic canvas
- ❑ Uniek Needloft plastic canvas yarn as listed in color key
- ❑ Red Heart Super Saver Art. E300 medium weight yarn as listed in color key
- ❑ Uniek Needloft metallic craft cord as listed in color key
- ❑ DMC 6-strand embroidery floss as listed in color key
- ❑ Eggshell sewing thread
- ❑ Ribbon:
  - ⅔ yard (.7m) ¼-inch-wide (7mm) eggshell satin ribbon
  - 1 yard (1m) ⅝-inch-wide (15mm) yellow-and-white gingham ribbon
- ❑ ⅜ yard (.4m) ½-inch-wide (12mm) eggshell ruffled lace trim
- ❑ Decorative buttons:
  - 2 (1-inch/2.5cm) LaMode sunflowers from Blumenthal Lansing
  - 1 Dress It Up bee from Jesse James Co.
- ❑ Complementary dish towel or hand towel
- ❑ Hand-sewing needle
- ❑ #16 tapestry needle

Project Note

Stitch using #16 tapestry needle unless instructed otherwise.

Stitching Step by Step

1 Cut front and back from plastic canvas according to graphs.

2 Stitch front and back according to graphs, filling in uncoded areas with tangerine Continental Stitches.

3 When background stitching is complete, Backstitch and Straight Stitch lid and "Honey" label using 3 strands dark coffee brown embroidery floss.

Embellishments & Finishing

1 Cut eggshell satin ribbon into 16-inch (.5m) and 8-inch (.25m) pieces. Referring to photo throughout, thread ends of longer piece through front from back to front where indicated by red dots on graph; tie ends in a bow on front; trim ends as desired. Tack bow in place with sewing needle and thread.

2 Thread ends of shorter piece through back from front to back; knot ends together on wrong side of back. Trim ends as needed.

3 With sewing needle and thread, stitch bee button to upper right corner of jar on topper front; stitch sunflower buttons to lower left edge of jar.

4 Using coffee and tangerine yarn, Overcast bottom edge of front and back according to graphs. Using coffee yarn throughout, Overcast top edges of front and back between arrows. Whipstitch front to back, wrong sides facing, along remaining edges.

5 With sewing needle and thread, stitch lace trim along bottom edge inside topper, turning under raw ends and trimming to fit.

6 Fold towel in half over center of ribbon; thread ribbon ends through towel topper from bottom to top and tie in a bow. Trim ribbon ends as needed.

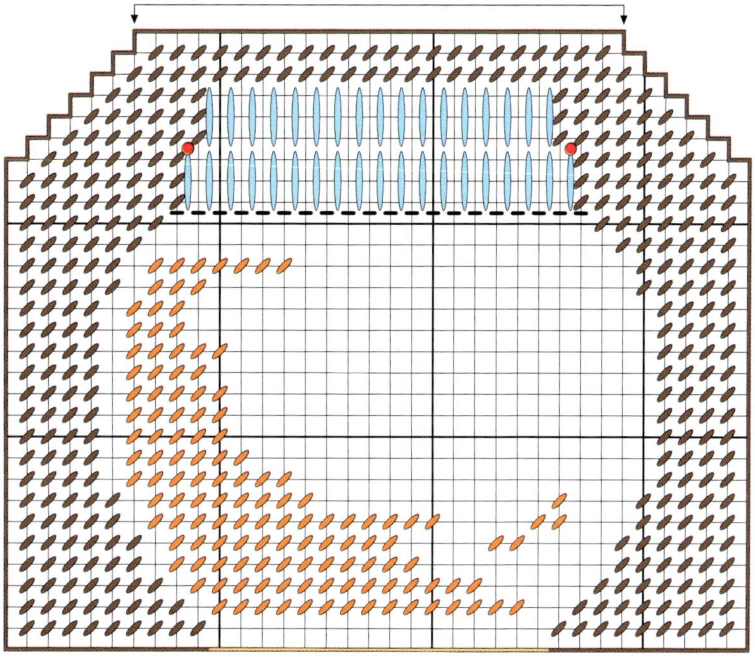

"Honey" Back
35 holes x 29 holes
Cut 1

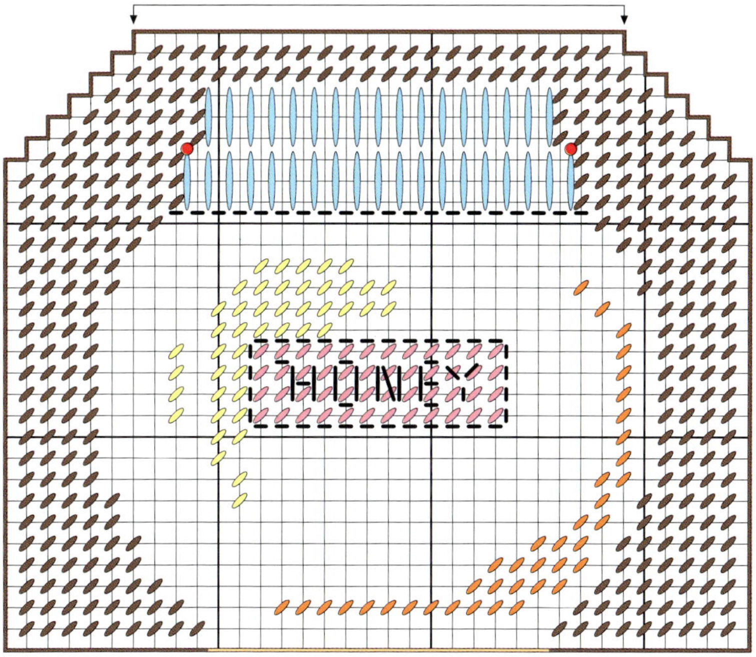

"Honey" Front
35 holes x 29 holes
Cut 1

COLOR KEY

Yards	Plastic Canvas Yarn
5 (4.6m)	Pumpkin #12
1 (1m)	Yellow #57
18 (16.5m)	Uncoded areas are tangerine #11 Continental Stitches
	Tangerine #11 Overcast
	Medium Weight Yarn
1 (1m)	Aran #313
18 (16.5m)	Coffee #365
	Metallic Craft Cord
5 (4.6m)	Gold #55001
	6-Strand Embroidery Floss
1 (1m)	Dark coffee brown #3371 (3-ply) Backstitch and Straight Stitch
	Attach ribbon

Color numbers given are for Uniek Needloft plastic canvas yarn and metallic craft cord, Red Heart Super Saver Art. E300 medium weight yarn and DMC 6-strand embroidery floss.

Apple

Size: 5⅜ inches W x 4½ inches H (13.6cm x 11.4cm) excluding ribbon hanger, towel and fringe
Skill Level: Beginner

Materials

- ❑ 1 sheet clear 7-count plastic canvas
- ❑ Uniek Needloft plastic canvas yarn as listed in color key
- ❑ Red Heart Super Saver Art. E300 medium weight yarn as listed in color key
- ❑ DMC 6-strand embroidery floss as listed in color key
- ❑ Sewing thread: green, ecru
- ❑ 1 yard (1m) ⅝-inch-wide (15mm) red-and-white stripe ribbon from Offray
- ❑ 2 Fashion Glass black briolettes from Cousin Corp.
- ❑ Complementary dish towel or hand towel
- ❑ Hand-sewing needle
- ❑ #16 tapestry needle

Project Note

Stitch using #16 tapestry needle unless instructed otherwise.

Stitching Step by Step

1 Cut two pieces for front and back, and three leaves from plastic canvas according to graphs.

2 Stitch front according to graph, filling in uncoded areas with Aran Continental Stitches.

3 When background stitching is complete, Straight Stitch apple stems using camel yarn; Backstitch between apples using 3 strands black embroidery floss.

4 Using sewing needle and ecru thread and referring to photo throughout, stitch briolettes to front for apple seeds.

5 Using black yarn, fill in back with Continental Stitches.

6 Stitch leaves according to graph. Overcast edges using light sage.

7 Using sewing needle and green thread, stitch base of leaves to apple stems as shown.

8 Referring to diagram for Lark's Head Knot, page 12, work Lark's Head Knots along bottom edge of front using 4-inch (10.2cm) strands of white yarn. Trim ends even.

Finishing

1 Using black yarn throughout, Overcast bottom edge of back; Overcast top edges of front and back between arrows. Whipstitch front to back, wrong sides facing, along remaining edges.

2 Fold towel in half over center of ribbon; thread ribbon ends through towel topper from bottom to top and tie in a bow. Trim ribbon ends as needed.

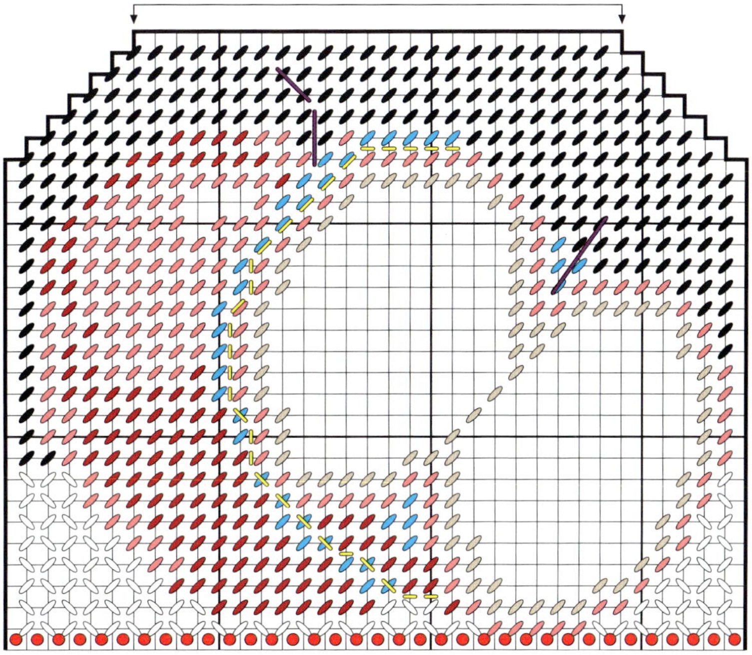

Apple Front/Back
35 holes x 29 holes
Cut 2
Stitch 1 as shown for front
Stitch 1 completely in black Continental Stitches for back

Apple Leaf
5 holes x 7 holes
Cut 3

COLOR KEY

Yards	Plastic Canvas Yarn
4 (3.7m)	Red #01
5 (4.6m)	Christmas red #02
2 (1.9m)	Burgundy #03
1 (1m)	Camel #43 Straight Stitch
	Medium Weight Yarn
9 (8.3m)	White #311
25 (22.9m)	Black #312
2 (1.9m)	Buff #334
2 (1.9m)	Frosty green #661
5 (4.6m)	Uncoded areas are Aran #313 Continental Stitches
1 (1m)	Light sage #631 Overcast
	White #311 Lark's Head Knot
	6-Strand Embroidery Floss
1 (1m)	Black #310 (3-ply) Backstitch

Color numbers given are for Uniek Needloft plastic canvas yarn, Red Heart Super Saver Art. E300 medium weight yarn and DMC 6-strand embroidery floss.

The Needlecraft Shop

Copyright © 2008 DRG,
306 East Parr Road,
Berne, IN 46711

ISBN: 978-1-57367-326-6
Printed in USA
1 2 3 4 5 6 7 8 9

Shopping for Supplies

For supplies, first shop your local craft and needlework stores. Some supplies may be found in fabric, hardware and discount stores. If you are unable to find the supplies you need, please call Annie's Attic at (800) 582-6643 to request a free catalog that sells plastic canvas supplies.

Getting Started

Before You Cut

Buy one brand of canvas for each entire project as brands can differ slightly in the distance between bars. Count holes carefully from the graph before you cut, using the bolder lines that show each 10 holes. These 10-count lines begin in the lower left corner of each graph to make counting easier. Mark canvas before cutting; then remove all marks completely before stitching. If the piece is cut in a rectangular or square shape and is either not worked, or worked with only one color and one type of stitch, the graph is not included in the pattern. Instead, the cutting and stitching instructions are given in the general instructions or with the individual project instructions.

Covering the Canvas

Bring needle up from back of work, leaving a short length of yarn on back of canvas; work over short length to secure. To end a thread, weave needle and thread through the wrong side of your last few stitches; clip. Follow the numbers on the small graphs beside each stitch illustration; bring your needle up from the back of the work on odd numbers and down through the front of the work on even numbers. Work embroidery stitches last, after the canvas has been completely covered by the needlepoint stitches.

Basic Stitches

Continental

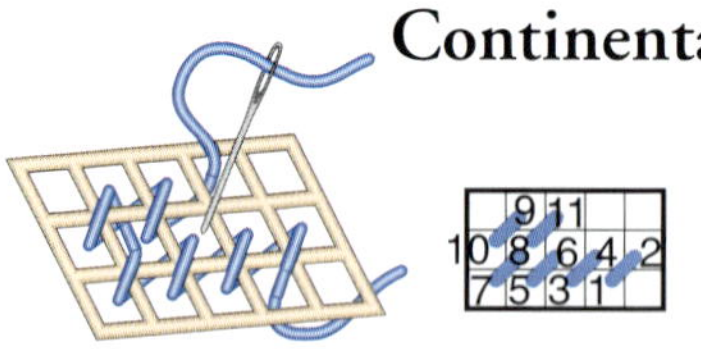

Overcast

Whipstitch

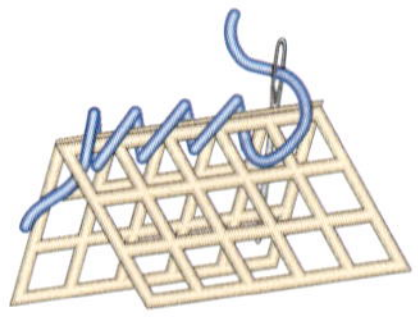

Slanted Gobelin

Long

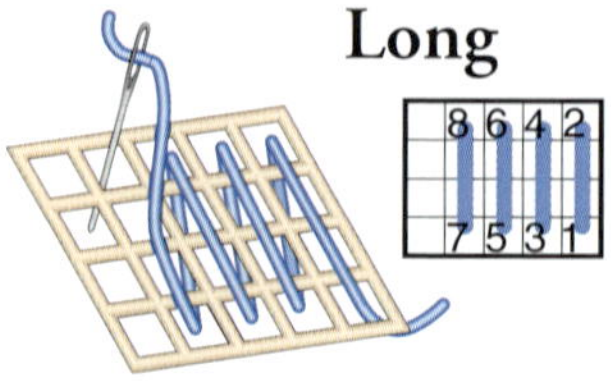

Cross

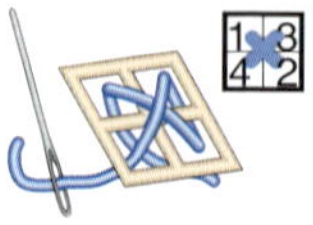

Embroidery Stitches

French Knot

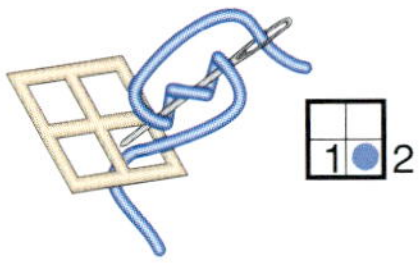

Lazy Daisy

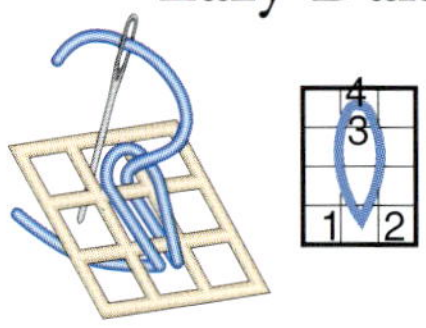

Backstitch

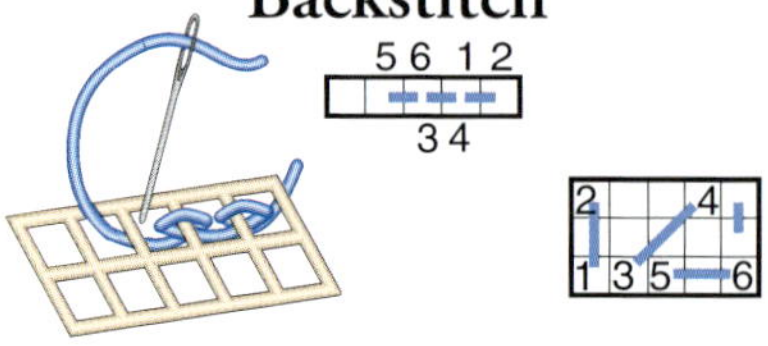

Straight

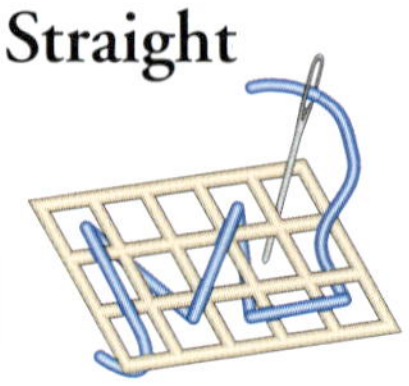

METRIC KEY:
millimeters = (mm)
centimeters = (cm)
meters = (m)
grams = (g)